This bool
those U
People who want to master
English language and
understand Tenses in the
easiest way possible

سُبْحَٰنَكَ لَا عِلْمَ لَنَآ اِلَّا مَا عَلَّمْتَنَا اِنَّكَ اَنْتَ الْعَلِيْمُ الْحَكِيْمُ

دل سے جو بات نکلتی ہے اثر رکھتی ہے   پر نہیں طاقت پرواز مگر رکھتی ہے
(حضرت علامہ محمد اقبالؒ)

The words spring from the heart surely carries weight,
though not endowed with wings;
it yet can fly in the space

(Hz.Allahmah Muhammad Iqbal Rah.)

To every problem there is already a solution,
whether you know it or not. To every sum in
there is already a correct answer, whether the
mathematician has found it or not.

(Grenville Kleiser)

Name of the book: Tenses English Urdu

Name of the author: Muhammad Sajid Ibrahim Meman

Address: Teacher, Jamiah Riyazul Uloom Academy, Kosamba.

Place: Kosamba, Gujarat, India.

Name of the publisher: Self Published

Year of Publication: January 2021

Other books by the same author:

The Mercy of Rahman to Memorise the holy Quran (Part 01 &02)

How to Memorise the holy Quran

Online Support

Email address: sm668161@gmail.com

Cellular Phone and Whatsapp no:+919428427819

YouTube Channel: Zillur Rahman Mutashabihatul Qur'an.

© Copyright Muhammad Sajid I Meman 2021

Preface

This humble is fortunate enough to teach English language to the students of Islamic seminaries for years. It has been my practice to teach my students Tenses in the easiest way possible. Alhamdulillah Almighty Allah had favoured this humble with the art of Tenses. The students who thoroughly studied tenses with me when met after years of graduation would thank me for the help I provided them to understand the Tenses.

So, it was my heartfelt desire to shape the lessons I taught to my students in the form pamphlets into a book which could serve Urdu speaking masses around the globe to easy understand the Tenses.

In this book I have solved the complexities of Tenses with a single example "eat" in all twelve Tenses and in all kinds of sentences positive, negative, interrogative and interrogative negative.

If Allah Almighty wills, you will discover in your hands a fabulous discovery! A marvelous mercy of Allah unto Mankind! A unique way of

presentation! A miraculous solution to have command over English language with
"Tenses English Urdu"

At last I thank Allah Almighty and Amazon Kindle who aided me in shaping this book, please do contact me on Email or WhatsApp if you have any queries or suggestions.

Do refer to your students and friends to read it for free on Kindle unlimited.

Yours sincerely,

Muhammad Sajid Ibrahim Meman,

Teacher, Jamiah Riyazul Uloom Academy,

Kosamba, Gujarat, India.

Contents

Online Support.. I
   Introduction to Tenses... 6
Let's begin 9
TENSES-زمانیں 9
SIMPLE PRESENT TENSE 9
Please refer the guidelines below for easy understanding... 10
PRESENT CONTINUOUS TENSE 11
PRESENT PERFECT TENSE 12
PRESENT PERFECT CONTINUOUS TENSE 14
SIMPLE PAST TENSE 17
PAST CONTINUOUS TENSE 18
PAST PERFECT TENSE 19
PAST PERFECT CONTINUOUS TENSE 21
SIMPLE FUTURE TENSE 23
FUTURE CONTINUOUS TENSE 25
FUTURE PERFECT TENSE... 27
FUTURE PERFECT CONTINUOUS TENSE 29
Tenses in a Nut-shell... 31

Passive voice 35
SIMPLE PRESENT TENSE 36
Present Continuous Tense 39
Present Perfect Tense 42
Past Tense 45
Simple Past Tense 45
Past Continuous Tense 48
Past Perfect Tense 51
Simple Future Tense 52
Future Perfect Tense 55
Forms of verb 58

Introduction to Tenses

In English grammar, verbs are often used in a way that it indicates or denotes the time when an event occurred. These verbs that take up different forms to indicate the time of an action, event or condition by changing its form are called as tenses. In other words Tenses play a crucial role in the English language. It denotes the time an action takes place, whether sometime in the past, in the present or will take some time in the future.

Tenses are broadly classified into three categories:

1. Present Tense
2. Past Tense
3. Future Tense

With each of these tenses, further classified into four other types

Present Tense

1. Simple Present Tense

2. Present continuous Tense

3. Present Perfect Tense

4. Present Perfect Continuous Tense

Past Tense

5. Simple Past Tense

6. Past continuous Tense

7. Past Perfect Tense

8. Past Perfect Continuous Tense

Future Tense

9. Simple Future Tense

10. Future continuous Tense

11. Future Perfect Tense

12. Future Perfect Continuous Tense

In this book we will learn all the Twelve Tenses with a single verb "eat" in all Tenses and in all types of sentences such as positive, negative, interrogative and interrogative negative and their transformations from active voice into passive voice.

Let's begin

TENSES-زمانیں

فعل: کھانا

Verb: eat

Different forms:(فعل کی مختلف شکلیں) eat, ate eaten

SIMPLE PRESENT TENSE

فعل حال مطلق (زنانہ حال مطلق)

Positive Sentences مثبتی جملے		Negative Sentences منفی جملے	
I, We, You, They	eat pizza. میں پڑا کھاتا ہوں۔	I, We, You They	do not eat pizza. میں پڑا نہیں کھاتا ہوں
He, She It	eat**S** pizza.	He She It	do**es** not eat pizza.

Interrogative Sentences سوالیہ جملے			Interrogative Negative سوالیہ منفی جملے		
Do	I, we, you, they	eat pizza ? کیا میں پڑا کھاتا ہوں؟	Do	I, we, you, they	not eat pizza ? کیا میں پڑا نہیں کھاتا ہوں؟
Does	He, she It	eat pizza ?	Does	he she it	not eat pizza ?

Please refer the guidelines below for easy understanding

ہدایات:۱- زمانہ حال مطلق میں فعل کی پہلی شکل eat کا استعمال ہو گا۔

۲- اس زمانہ میں معمول یا عادت کے طور پر کیے جانے والے کاموں کو بتایا جاتا ہے۔

۳- اس زمانہ میں سوالیہ، منفی، اور سوالیہ منفی جملوں میں do اور does کا استعمال ہوتا ہے۔

۴- زمانہ حال مطلق میں he, she, it میں فعل کے پیچھے "s" بڑھایا جاتا ہے۔

تنبیہ: eat کے پیچھے "s" بڑھانے سے "eats" ہو جائیگا اور اگر کسی فعل کے اخیر میں "sh" "ch" "x" "s" "o" ہو تو "s" کے بجائے "es" لگایا جائیگا۔

۵- میں پڑا کھاتا ہوں یعنی مجھے پڑا پسند ہے اور میں اسے کھاتا ہوں یہ معنی ہوتے ہیں۔

۶- فی الحال میں آپ سے بات کر رہا ہوں اور پڑا کھانے کا فعل جاری نہیں ہے۔

PRESENT CONTINUOUS TENSE

<u>فعل حال جاری</u> (زنانہ حال استمراری)

Positive Sentences مثبتی جملے		Negative Sentences منفی جملے	
I	**am eating pizza.** میں پڑا کھا رہا ہوں۔	I	am not eating pizza. میں پڑا نہیں کھا رہا ہوں۔
We, You, They	**are eating pizza.**	We, You, They	are not eating pizza.
He, She, It	**is eating pizza.**	He, She, It	is not eating pizza.

Interrogative Sentences سوالیہ جملے			Interrogative Negative سوالیہ منفی جملے		
Am	I	**eating pizza ?** کیا میں پڑا کھا رہا ہوں؟	Am	I	not eating pizza? کیا میں پڑا نہیں کھا رہا ہوں؟
Are	**we you they**	eating pizza ?	Are	we you they	not eating pizza ?
Is	he, she, it	eating pizza ?	Is	He, she, It	not eating pizza ?

ہدایات: ۱ـ زمانہ حال استمراری میں فعل کی پہلی شکل کا استعمال ہو گا اور اس کے پیچھے ing لگایا جائیگا۔

۲ـ اس زمانہ میں پزا کھانے کا فعل فی الحال جاری ہے یہ بتایا جا رہا ہے (میں آپ سے بات کرتے کرتے پزّا بھی کھا رہا ہوں)۔

۳ـ ing کے معنی ہے رہا، رہی یا رہے ہوتا ہے۔

PRESENT PERFECT TENSE

فعل حال مکمل (زنانہ حال مکمل یا ماضی قریب)

Please refer the guidelines below the tables for easy understanding

Positive Sentences مثبتی جملے		Negative Sentences منفی جملے	
I, We, You They	have eaten pizza. میں نے پزّا کھایا ہے۔	I, We, You They	have not eaten pizza. میں نے پزّا نہیں کھایا ہے۔
He, She It	has eaten pizza.	He, She It	has not eaten pizza.

Interrogative Sentences سوالیہ جملے			Interrogative Negative سوالیہ منفی جملے		
Have	I, we, you, they	eaten pizza? کیا میں نے پڑا کھایا ہے؟	Have	I, we, you, they	not eaten pizza? کیا میں نے پڑا نہیں کھایا ہے؟
Has	he, she it	eaten pizza?	Has	he, she it	not eaten pizza?

ہدایات:- ا__ زمانہ حال مکمل میں فعل کی تیسری شکل (eaten) کا استعمال ہوتا ہے۔

۲__ اس زمانہ میں پڑا کھانے کا فعل ابھی ابھی پورا ہوا ہے (میں نے آپ سے بات کرنے سے تھوڑی دیر پہلے پڑا کھایا ہے)۔

۳__ زمانہ حال مکمل میں I, we you, they کے ساتھ (have) کا استعمال ہوتا ہے،اور he, she, it کے ساتھ (has) کا استعمال ہوتا ہے۔

۴__ have اور has کے معنی "ہے" یا "ہیں"۔ کے ہوتے ہے۔

13

PRESENT PERFECT CONTINUOUS TENSE

<u>فعل حال مکمل جاری</u> (زنانہ حال مکمل استمراری)

✓ **Please refer the guidelines below the tables for easy understanding**

Positive Sentences مثبتی جملے		Negative Sentences منفی جملے	
I, We You, They	have been eating pizza since 8:30 a.m./ for half an Hour.	I, We You, They	have not been eating pizza Since 8:30 a.m. / for half an Hour.
He, She It	or has been eating pizza since 8:30 a.m./ for half an Hour. میں ۸۔۳۰ سے (یا آدھے گھنٹے سے) پڑا کھا رہا ہوں۔	He, She It	or has not been eating pizza since 8:30 a.m./for Half an Hour. میں ۸۔۳۰ سے (یا آدھے گھنٹے سے) پڑا نہیں کھا رہا ہوں۔

14

Interrogative Sentences سوالیہ جملے			Interrogative Negative Sentences سوالیہ منفی جملے		
Have	I we you they	been eating pizza since 8:30 a.m? or been eating pizza for half an hour ? کیا میں ۸:۳۰ سے (یا آدھے گھنٹے سے) پڑا کھا رہا ہوں؟	Have	I we you they	not been eating pizza since 8:30 a.m ? or not been eating pizza for half an hour ? کیا میں ۸:۳۰ سے (یا آدھے گھنٹے سے) پڑا نہیں کھا رہا ہوں؟
Has	he she it		Has	he she it	

ہدایات:

۱؎ زمانہ حال مکمل استمراری میں I,we you,they کے ساتھ (have been) کا استعمال ہوتا ہے، اور he,she,it کے ساتھ (has been) کا استعمال ہوتا ہے۔

۲؎ زمانہ حال مکمل استمراری میں فعل کی پہلی شکل کا استعمال ہوتا ہے اور اس کے پیچھے ing لگایا جائیگا۔

۳؎ اس زمانہ میں پڑھ اکھانے کا فعل کچھ وقت پہلے شروع ہوا اور ابھی جاری ہے (میں آپ سے ۸۔۳۰ سے بات کرتے کرتے پڑھ اکھا رہا ہوں اور فی الحال بھی پڑھنا کھانا جاری ہے)۔

۴؎ زمانہ حال مکمل استمراری میں "since" یا "for" کا استعمال ہوتا ہے، "since" یا "for" کے معنی "سے" ۔"کے ہوتے ہے۔

۵؎ "since" کا استعمال طے وقت بتانے کے لیے اور "for" کا استعمال مدت بتانے کے لیے ہوتا ہے۔

SIMPLE PAST TENSE

فعل ماضی مطلق (زنانہ ماضی مطلق)

Please refer the guidelines below the tables for easy understanding

Positive Sentences مثبتی جملے		Negative Sentences منفی جملے	
I, We You, He She, It They	ate pizza. میں نے پڑا کھایا۔	I, We You, He She, It They	did not eat pizza. میں نے پڑا نہیں کھایا۔

Interrogative Sentences سوالیہ جملے			Interrogative Negative سوالیہ منفی جملے		
Did	I, we you, he she, it they	eat pizza ? کیا میں نے پڑا کھایا؟	Did	I, we you, he she, it they	not eat pizza ? کیا میں نے پڑا نہیں کھایا؟

ہدایات: ١- زمانہ ماضی مطلق میں I,we you, he she,it,they سبھی کے ساتھ فعل کی دوسری شکل (ate) کا استعمال ہوتا ہے۔

٢- اس زمانہ میں پزا کھانے کا فعل پورا ہو نے کی جانکاری ہے (میں نے پزا کھایا)

٣- زمانہ ماضی مطلق کے صرف مثبتی جملوں میں فعل کی دوسری شکل "ate" کا استعمال ہوتا ہے۔

٤- زمانہ ماضی مطلق کے بقیہ جملوں میں (یعنی منفی، سوالیہ، اور سوالیہ منفی جملوں میں) فعل کی پہلی شکل "eat" کا استعمال ہوتا ہے اور "do" کا ماضی "did" کا استعمال ہوتا ہے۔

PAST CONTINUOUS TENSE

فعل ماضی جاری (زنانہ ماضی استمراری)

Please refer the guidelines below the tables for easy understanding

Positive Sentences مثبتی جملے		Negative Sentences منفی جملے	
I, He, She, It	was eating pizza. میں پزا کھا رہا تھا۔	I, He, She, It	was not eating pizza. میں پزا نہیں کھا رہا تھا۔
We, You They	were eating pizza.	We, You They	were not eating pizza.

Interrogative Sentences سوالیہ جملے			Interrogative Negative سوالیہ منفی جملے		
Was	I, he she, it	eating pizza ? کیا میں پڑّا کھا رہا تھا؟	Was	I, he She, it	not eating pizza ? کیا میں پڑّا نہیں کھا رہا تھا؟
Were	we you they	^	Were	we you they	^

ہدایات:- ا زمانہ ماضی استمراری میں I,he,she,it کے ساتھ (was) کا استعمال ہوتا ہے، اور we,you,they کے ساتھ (were) کا استعمال ہوتا ہے۔

٢- زمانہ ماضی استمراری میں فعل کی پہلی شکل کا استعمال ہوتا ہے اور اس کے پیچھے ing لگایا جائیگا۔

٣- اس زمانہ میں ماضی میں کام کے جاری رہنے کی جانکاری ہے (یعنی پڑا کھانے کا فعل ماضی میں جاری ہے)

٤- ing کے معنی ہے رہا، رہی یا رہے۔

PAST PERFECT TENSE

فعل ماضی مکمل (زنانہ ماضی مکمل یا ماضی بعید)

Please refer the guidelines below the tables for easy understanding

19

Positive Sentences مثبتی جملے		Negative Sentences منفی جملے	
I, We, You, He, She, It They	had eaten pizza. میں نے پڑا کھایا تھا۔	I, We, You, He, She, It They	had not eaten pizza. میں نے پڑا نہیں کھایا تھا۔

Interrogative Sentences سوالیہ جملے			Interrogative Negative سوالیہ منفی جملے		
Had	I, we, you, he, she, it they	eaten pizza ? کیا میں نے پڑا کھایا تھا؟	Had	I, we, you, he, she, it they	not eaten pizza ? کیا میں نے پڑا نہیں کھایا تھا؟

ہدایات:۱۔ زمانہ ماضی مکمل (یا ماضی بعید) میں I,we you,they,he she,it سبھی کے ساتھ had کا استعمال ہوتا ہے (جو کہ have اور has کا ماضی ہے)۔

۲۔ زمانہ ماضی مکمل میں فعل کی تیسری شکل (eaten) کا استعمال ہوتا ہے۔

تنبیہ: تینوں perfect زمانوں میں (یعنی present perfect, past perfect, اور future perfect) میں فعل کی تیسری شکل (eaten) کا استعمال ہوتا ہے۔

۱۳۔ اس زمانہ میں پزا کھانے کا فعل کافی مدت پہلے پورا ہو چکا تھا (میں نے پزا بہت وقت پہلے کھایا تھا)۔

۲۔ had کے معنی "تھا" یا "تھے" کے ہوتے ہے۔

PAST PERFECT CONTINUOUS TENSE

فعل ماضی مکمل جاری (زنانہ ماضی مکمل استمراری)

Positive Sentences مثبتی جملے	Negative Sentences منفی جملے
I We You He She It They	had been eating pizza since 8:30 a.m. OR had been eating pizza for half an hour. میں ۸:۳۰ سے (یا آدھے گھنٹے سے) پزا کھا رہا تھا۔	I We You He She It They	had not been eating pizza since 8:30 a.m. OR had not been eating pizza for half an hour. میں ۸:۳۰ سے (یا آدھے گھنٹے سے) پزا نہیں کھا رہا تھا۔

21

Interrogative Sentences سوالیہ جملے			Interrogative Negative سوالیہ منفی جملے		
Had	I we you he she it they	been eating pizza since 8:30 a.m? OR been eating pizza for half an hour ? کیا میں ۸:۳۰ سے (یا آدھے گھنٹے سے) پزّا کھا رہا تھا؟	Had	I we you he she it they	not been eating pizza since 8:30 a.m? OR not been eating pizza for half an hour ? کیا میں ۸:۳۰ سے (یا آدھے گھنٹے سے) پزّا نہیں کھا رہا تھا؟

ہدایات:۔۱ زمانہ ماضی مکمل استمراری میں I, we you, he, she, it, they سبھی کے ساتھ had been کا استعمال ہوتا ہے (جو کہ have been اور has been کا ماضی ہے)۔

۲۔ زمانہ ماضی مکمل استمراری میں فعل کی پہلی شکل کا استعمال ہوتا ہے اور اس کے پیچھے ing لگایا جائیگا۔

۳۔ اس زمانہ میں پزا کھانے کا فعل ماضی میں کچھ وقت پہلے شروع ہوا اور ماضی میں جاری رہنے کی جانکاری ہے۔ (میں آپ سے ۸ سے ۳۰ سے بات کرتے کرتے پزا کھا رہا تھا)۔

۴۔ زمانہ ماضی مکمل استمراری میں "since" یا "for" کا استعمال ہوتا ہے، "since" یا "for" کے معنی "سے" کے ہوتے ہے۔

۵۔ "since" کا استعمال طے وقت بتانے کے لیے اور "for" کا استعمال مدت بتانے کے لیے ہوتا ہے۔

SIMPLE FUTURE TENSE

فعل مستقبل مطلق (زنانہ مستقبل مطلق)

Positive Sentences مثبتی جملے		Negative Sentences منفی جملے	
I We	**shall eat pizza.** میں پزا کھاؤنگا۔	I We	shall not eat pizza. میں پزا نہیں کھاؤنگا۔
You He She It They	**will eat pizza.**	You He She It They	will not eat pizza.

23

Interrogative Sentences سوالیہ جملے			Interrogative Negative سوالیہ منفی جملے		
Shall	I We	eat pizza ?	Shall	I we	not eat pizza ?
Will	you he she it They	کیا میں پزّا کھاؤں گا؟	Will	you he she it they	کیا میں پزّا نہیں کھاؤں گا؟

ہدایات :۱ـ زمانہ مستقبل مطلق میں I,we کے ساتھ (shall) کا استعمال ہوتا ہے، اور you,he,she,it,they کے ساتھ (will) کا استعمال ہوتا ہے۔

۲ـ shall اور will کے معنی "گا، گے، گی" کے ہوتے ہیں۔

۳ـ زمانہ مستقبل مطلق میں فعل کی پہلی شکل (eat) کا استعمال ہوتا ہے۔

۴ـ اس زمانہ میں کام کے مستقبل میں ہونے کی جانکاری ہوتی ہے۔

۵ـ جدید انگریزی میں I, we کے ساتھ بھی (will) کا استعمال ہونے لگا ہے۔

FUTURE CONTINUOUS TENSE

<u>فعل مستقبل جاری</u> (زنانہ مستقبل استمراری)

Please refer the guidelines below the tables for easy understanding

Positive Sentences مشبتی جملے		Negative Sentences منفی جملے	
I We	**shall be** eating pizza. میں پڑا کھاتا ہو نگا۔	I We	shall not be eating pizza. میں پڑا نہیں کھاتا ہو نگا۔
You He She It They	**will be** eating pizza.	You He She It They	will not be eating pizza.

Interrogative Sentences سوالیہ جملے			Interrogative Negative سوالیہ منفی جملے		
Shall	I We	be eating pizza ? کیا میں پڑا کھا تا رہوں گا؟	Shall	I we	not be eating pizza ? کیا میں پڑا نہیں کھا تا رہوں گا؟
Will	you he she it they	be eating pizza ?	Will	you he she it they	not be eating pizza ?

ہدایات:۔1 زمانہ مستقبل استمراری میں I,we کے ساتھ (shall be) کا استعمال ہوتا ہے، اور you,he,she,it,they کے ساتھ (will be) کا استعمال ہوتا ہے۔

2۔ shall be اور will be کے معنی گا، گے، گی کے ہوتے ہیں۔ (یعنی تا رہوں گا کے ہوتے ہیں)

3۔ زمانہ مستقبل استمراری میں فعل کی پہلی شکل (eat) کا استعمال ہوتا ہے اور اس کے پیچھے ing لگایا جائیگا۔

ع۔ اس زمانہ میں پزا کھانے کا فعل مستقبل میں جاری رہنے کی جانکاری ہے۔ (میں آپ سے بات کرتے کرتے پزا مستقبل میں کھاتا رہوں گا)۔

FUTURE PERFECT TENSE

فعل مستقبل مکمل (زنانہ مستقبل مکمل)

✓ **Please refer the guidelines below the tables for easy understanding**

Positive Sentences مثبتی جملے			Negative Sentences منفی جملے		
I We	Shall	have eaten pizza. میں پزا کھالوں گا۔ یا کھا چکوں گا۔	I We	shall	have not eaten pizza. میں پزا نہیں کھالوں گا۔ یا کھا چکوں گا۔
You He She It They	Will		You He She It They	will	

Interrogative Sentences سوالیہ جملے			Interrogative Negative سوالیہ منفی جملے		
Shall	I We	have eaten pizza ? کیا میں پڑّا کھاؤں گا؟	Shall	I we	have not eaten pizza ? کیا میں پڑّا نہیں کھاؤں گا؟
Will	you he she it they		Will	you he she it they	

ہدایات: ۱- زمانہ مستقبل مکمل میں I, we کے ساتھ (shall have) کا استعمال ہوتا ہے، اور you, he, she, it, they کے ساتھ (will have) کا استعمال ہوتا ہے۔

۲- زمانہ مستقبل مکمل میں فعل کی تیسری شکل (eaten) کا استعمال ہوتا ہے۔

تنبیہ: تینوں perfect زمانوں میں (یعنی present perfect, past perfect, اور future perfect) میں فعل کی تیسری شکل (eaten) کا استعمال ہوتا ہے۔

۳- اس زمانہ میں پزا کھانے کا فعل مستقبل میں پورا ہو جانے کی جانکاری ہے۔

۴- shall have, will have کے معنی "لوں گا" کے ہوتے ہیں۔

FUTURE PERFECT CONTINUOUS TENSE

فعل مستقبل مکمل جاری (زنانہ مستقبل مکمل استمرای)

Positive Sentences مثبتی جملے			Negative Sentences منفی جملے		
I We	Shall	have been eating pizza Since 8:30 a.m. (or for half an hour.) میں ۸:۳۰ سے (یا آدھے گھنٹے سے) پڑا کھار ہاہونگا۔	I We	Shall	have not been eating pizza Since 8:30 a.m. (or for half an hour) میں ۸:۳۰ سے (یا آدھے گھنٹے سے) پڑا نہیں کھار ہاہونگا۔
You They He She It	Will		You They He She It	Will	

Interrogative Sentences سوالیہ جملے			Interrogative Negative سوالیہ منفی جملے		
Shall	I We	have been eating pizza Since 8:30 a.m. (or for half an Hour)?	Shall	I we	have not been eating pizza Since 8:30 a.m. (or for half an Hour)?
Will	you he she it they		Will	you he she it they	

کیا میں ۸:۳۰ سے (یا آدھے گھنٹے سے) پڑّا کھا رہا ہوگا؟

کیا میں ۸:۳۰ سے (یا آدھے گھنٹے سے) پڑّا نہیں کھا رہا ہوگا؟

ہدایات: ۱- زمانہ مستقبل مکمل استمراری میں I,we کے ساتھ (shall have been) کا استعمال ہوتا ہے،اور you,he,she,it,they کے ساتھ (will have been) کا استعمال ہوتا ہے۔

۲- زمانہ مستقبل مکمل استمراری میں فعل کی پہلی شکل کا استعمال ہوتا ہے اور اس کے پیچھے ing لگایا جائیگا۔

۳- اس زمانہ میں پڑا کھانے کا فعل مستقبل میں کچھ وقت سے کچھ وقت کے بیچ جاری رہنے کی جانکاری ہے۔

۴- زمانہ مستقبل مکمل استمراری میں "since" یا "for" کا استعمال ہوتا ہے، "since" یا "for" کے معنی "سے" کے ہوتے ہے۔

۵- "since" کا استعمال طے وقت بتانے کے لیے اور "for" کا استعمال مدت بتانے کے لیے ہوتا ہے۔

Tenses in a Nut-shell

زمانوں کا مختصر خلاصہ

فعل: کھانا

Verb: eat

Different forms: (فعل کی مختلف شکلیں) eat, ate eaten

Note: Students are requested to memorise the example given below in a nutshell for future reference.

	Present Tense	
Simple Present Tense	I, We, You, They eat pizza. He, She, It eat<u>s</u> pizza.	میں پڑا کھاتا ہوں۔
Present Continuous Tense	I am eat<u>ing</u> pizza. He, She, It is <u>eating</u> pizza. We, You, They are <u>eating</u> pizza.	میں پڑا کھا رہا ہوں۔
Present Perfect Tense	I, We, You, They have <u>eaten</u> pizza. He, She, It has <u>eaten</u> pizza.	میں نے پڑا کھایا ہے۔
Present Perfect Continuous	I, We, You, They <u>have been eating</u> pizza for half an hour/ since 8:30	میں آدھے گھنٹے سے (یا)

Tense	a.m. He, She, It has been eating pizza for half an hour/ since 8:30 a.m.	پڑا (۸۔۳۰ سے) کھا رہا ہوں۔
Past Tense		
Simple Past Tense	I, We, You, They, He, She, It ate pizza.	میں نے پڑا کھایا۔
Past Continuous Tense	I, He, She, It was eating pizza. We, You, They were eating pizza.	میں پڑا کھا رہا تھا۔
Past Perfect Tense	I, We, You, They, He She, It had eaten pizza.	میں نے پڑا کھایا تھا۔
Past Perfect Continuous Tense	I, We, You, They, He She, It had been eating pizza for half an hour/ since 8:30 a.m.	میں ۸۔۳۰ سے (یا آدھے گھنٹے سے) پڑا کھا رہا تھا۔
Future Tense		
Simple Future Tense	I, We shall eat pizza. You, They, He, She, It will eat pizza.	میں پڑا کھاؤں گا۔

Future Continuous Tense	I, We shall be eating pizza. You, They, He, She, It will be eating pizza.	میں پڑا کھاتا رہوں گا۔
Future Perfect Tense	I, We shall have eaten pizza. You, They, He, She, It will have eaten pizza.	میں پڑا کھا لوں گا۔ یا کھا چکوں گا۔
Future Perfect Continuous Tense	I, We, shall have been eating pizza for half an hour/ since 8:30 a.m. You, They, He, She, It will have been eating pizza for half an hour/ since 8:30 a.m.	میں 8۔30 سے (یا آدھے گھنٹے سے) پڑا کھا رہا ہوں گا۔

Passive voice

فعلِ مجہول

<u>Active and Passive voice:</u> Words come together to form a sentence and these sentences can be formed in more than one way. The way these sentences are made make a lot of difference in writing. One thing to note here is that no matter what the structure of the sentence is, the meaning of the sentence does not change. That's actually a very important point to remember throughout the study of Active and Passive Voice.

Note: Out of twelve Tenses, only the transformation of eight Tenses into passive voice is possible let's solve the same example in Passive Voice

✓ صرف آٹھ ہی زمانوں میں فعلِ معروف (Active voice) سے فعلِ مجہول (Passive voice) میں تبدیل کیا جا سکتا ہے چلیں شروع کرتے ہیں۔

فعل: کھانا

Verb: eat

Different forms(فعل کی مختلف شکلیں) : eat, ate eaten

SIMPLE PRESENT TENSE

فعل حال مطلق

ہدایات:۱۔ فعلِ مجہول(Passive voice) کے سبھی زمانوں میں فعل کی تیسری شکل (eaten) کا استعمال ہو گا۔

۲۔ فعلِ مجہول(Passive voice) کے سبھی زمانوں میں میں فاعل کو مفعول کی جگہ پر اور مفعول کو فاعل کی جگہ پر رکھا جاتا ہے اور اس سے پہلے by لگایا جاتا ہے۔

۳۔ (Passive voice) کے سبھی زمانوں میں I کو me میں we کو us میں he کو him میں she کو her میں they کو them میں میں تبدیل کیا جاتا۔

۴۔ اس زمانہ میں مفعول واحد ہو تو اس کے بعد is اور جمع ہو تو are کا استعمال ہوتا ہے۔

Positive Sentences مثبتی جملے		Negative Sentences منفی جملے	
Active Voice فعلِ معروف	Passive Voice فعلِ مجہول	Active Voice فعلِ معروف	Passive Voice فعلِ مجہول
I, We, You, They eat pizza. میں پزّا کھاتا ہوں۔	Pizza is eaten by me. (us, you, him, her, it, them) پزّا مجھ سے کھایا جاتا ہے۔ (اگر پزّا جمع ہو)	I, We, You They do not eat pizza. میں پزّا نہیں کھاتا ہوں۔	Pizza is not eaten by me. (us, you, him, her, it, them) پزّا مجھ سے نہیں کھایا جاتا ہے۔ (اگر پزّا جمع ہو)
He, She It eatS pizza.	Pizzas are eaten by me. (us, you, him, her, it, them) پزّا مجھ سے کھائے جاتے ہیں۔	He She It doeS not eat pizza.	Pizzas are not eaten by me. (us, you, him, her, it, them) پزّا مجھ سے نہیں کھائے جاتے ہیں۔

Interrogative Sentences سوالیہ جملے		Interrogative Negative سوالیہ منفی جملے	
Active Voice فعلِ معروف	Passive Voice فعلِ مجہول	Active Voice فعلِ معروف	Passive Voice فعلِ مجہول
Do I, We, You, They eat pizza? کیا میں پڑا کھاتا ہوں؟	**Is pizza eaten by me?** (us, you, him, her, it, them) کیا پڑا مجھ سے کھایا جاتا ہے؟	Do I, We, You, They not eat pizza? کیا میں پڑا نہیں کھاتا ہوں؟	Is pizza not eaten by me? (us, you, him, her, it, them) کیا پڑا مجھ سے نہیں کھایا جاتا ہے؟
Does he, she it eat pizza?	(اگر پزا جمع ہو) **Are pizzas eaten by me?** (us, you, him, her, it, them) کیا پڑا مجھ سے کھائے جاتے ہیں؟	Does he, she, it not eat pizza?	(اگر پزا جمع ہو) Are pizzas not eaten by me? (us, you, him, her, it, them) کیا پڑا مجھ سے نہیں کھائے جاتے ہیں؟

Present Continuous Tense

فعل حال جاری

ہدایات: ۱۔ فعلِ مجہول (Passive voice) کے سبھی زمانوں میں فعل کی تیسری شکل (eaten) کا استعمال ہو گا۔

۲۔ اس زمانہ میں مفعول واحد کے ساتھ is being اور جمع فعل کے ساتھ are being کا استعمال ہوتا ہے۔

۳۔ (Passive voice) کے سبھی زمانوں میں I کو me میں we کو us میں he کو him میں she کو her میں they کو them میں تبدیل کیا جاتا۔

Positive Sentences مثبتی جملے		Negative Sentences منفی جملے	
Active Voice فعلِ معروف	Passive Voice فعلِ مجہول	Active Voice فعلِ معروف	Passive Voice فعلِ مجہول
I am eating pizza. میں پزّا کھا رہا ہوں۔ We, You, They are eating pizza. ہم پزّا کھا رہے ہیں۔ He, She, It is eating pizza. وہ پزّا کھا رہا ہے۔	Pizza is being eaten by me. (us, you, him, her, it, them) پزّا مجھ سے کھایا جا رہا ہے۔ (اگر پزّا جمع ہو) Pizzas are being eaten by me. (us, you, him, her, it, them) پزّا مجھ سے کھائے جا رہے ہیں۔	I am not eating pizza. We, You, They are not eating pizza. میں پزّا نہیں کھا رہا ہوں۔ ہم پزّا نہیں کھا رہے ہیں He, She, It is not eating pizza. وہ پزّا نہیں کھا رہا ہے۔	Pizza is not being eaten by me. (us, you, him, her, it, them) پزّا مجھ سے نہیں کھایا جا رہا ہے۔ (اگر پزّا جمع ہو) Pizzas are not being eaten by me. (us, you, him, her, it, them) پزّا مجھ سے کھائے جا رہے ہیں۔

Interrogative Sentences سوالیہ جملے		Interrogative Negative سوالیہ منفی جملے	
Active Voice فعلِ معروف	Passive Voice فعلِ مجہول	Active Voice فعلِ معروف	Passive Voice فعلِ مجہول
Am I eating pizza? Are we, you, they eating pizza? کیا میں پڑا کھا رہا ہوں؟ کیا ہم پڑا کھا رہے ہیں؟	Is pizza being eaten by me? (us, you, him, her, it, them) کیا پڑا مجھ سے کھایا جا رہا ہے؟ (اگر پڑا جمع ہو) Are pizzas being eaten by me? (us, you, him, her, it, them) کیا پڑا مجھ سے کھائے جا رہے ہیں؟	Am I not eating pizza? Are we, you, they not eating pizza? کیا میں پڑا نہیں کھا رہا ہوں؟ کیا ہم پڑا نہیں کھا رہے ہیں؟	Is pizza being not eaten by me? (us, you, him, her, it, them) کیا مجھ سے پڑا نہیں کھایا جا رہا ہے؟ (اگر پڑا جمع ہو) Are pizzas being not eaten by me? (us, you, him, her, it, them) کیا پڑا مجھ سے نہیں کھائے جا رہے ہیں؟
Is he, she, it eating pizza? کیا وہ پڑا کھا رہا ہے؟		Is he, she, it not eating pizza? کیا وہ پڑا نہیں کھا رہا ہے؟	

Present Perfect Tense

فعل حال مکمل

ہدایات: ۱۔ فعلِ مجہول (Passive voice) کے سبھی زمانوں میں فعل کی تیسری شکل (eaten) کا استعمال ہو گا۔

۲۔ اس زمانہ میں مفعول واحد کے ساتھ has been اور جمع مفعول کے ساتھ have been کا استعمال ہوتا ہے۔

۳۔ (Passive voice) کے سبھی زمانوں میں I کو me میں we کو us میں he کو him میں she کو her میں they کو them میں تبدیل کیا جاتا۔

Positive Sentences مثبتی جملے		Negative Sentences منفی جملے	
Active Voice فعلِ معروف	Passive Voice فعلِ مجہول	Active Voice فعلِ معروف	Passive Voice فعلِ مجہول
I, We, You, They have eaten pizza. میں نے پڑا کھایا ہے۔	**Pizza has been eaten by me.** (us, you, him, her, it, them) پڑا مجھ سے کھایا گیا ہے۔ (اگر پڑا جمع ہو)	I, We, You, They have not eaten pizza. میں نے پڑا نہیں کھایا ہے۔	Pizza has not been eaten by me. (us, you, him, her, it, them) پڑا مجھ سے نہیں کھایا گیا ہے۔ (اگر پڑا جمع ہو)
He, She, It is has eaten pizza. اس نے پڑا کھایا ہے۔	**Pizzas have been eaten by me.** (us, you, him, her, it, them) پڑا مجھ سے کھائے گئے ہیں۔	He, She, It is has not eaten pizza. اس نے پڑا نہیں کھایا ہے۔	Pizzas have not been eaten by me. (us, you, him, her, it, them) پڑا مجھ سے نہیں کھائے گئے ہیں۔

Interrogative Sentences سوالیہ جملے		Interrogative Negative سوالیہ منفی جملے	
Active Voice فعلِ معروف	Passive Voice فعلِ مجہول	Active Voice فعلِ معروف	Passive Voice فعلِ مجہول
Have I, we, you, they eaten pizza? کیا میں نے پزا کھایا ہے؟	Has pizza been eaten by me? (us, you, him, her, it, them) کیا پزا مجھ سے کھایا گیا ہے؟ (اگر پزا جمع ہو)	Have I, we, you, they not eaten pizza? کیا میں نے پزا نہیں کھایا ہے؟	Has pizza been not eaten by me? (us, you, him, her, it, them) کیا پزا مجھ سے کھایا نہیں گیا ہے؟ (اگر پزا جمع ہو)
Has he, she, it eaten pizza? کیا اس نے پزا کھایا ہے؟	Have pizzas been eaten by me? (us, you, him, her, it, them) کیا پزا مجھ سے کھائے گئے ہیں؟	Has he, she, it not eaten pizza? کیا اس نے پزا نہیں کھایا ہے؟	Have pizzas been not eaten by me? (us, you, him, her, it, them) کیا پزا مجھ سے نہیں کھائے گئے ہیں؟

Past Tense

Simple Past Tense

<u>فعل ماضی مطلق (زنانہ ماضی مطلق)</u>

ہدایات:۱۔ فعل مجہول (Passive voice) کے سبھی زمانوں میں فعل کی تیسری شکل (eaten) کا استعمال ہو گا۔

۲۔ اس زمانہ میں مفعول واحد کے ساتھ was اور جمع مفعول کے ساتھ were کا استعمال ہوتا ہے۔

۳۔ (Passive voice) کے سبھی زمانوں میں I کو me میں we کو us میں he کو him میں she کو her میں they کو them میں میں تبدیل کیا جاتا۔

Positive Sentences مثبتی جملے		Negative Sentences منفی جملے	
Active Voice فعلِ معروف	**Passive Voice** فعلِ مجہول	**Active Voice** فعلِ معروف	Passive Voice فعلِ مجہول
I, We, You, They, He, She, It ate pizza. میں نے پڑا کھایا۔	Pizza was eaten by me. (us, you, him, her, it, them) پڑا مجھ سے کھایا گیا۔ (اگر پڑا جمع ہو) Pizzas were eaten by me. (us, you, him, her, it, them) پڑا مجھ سے کھائے گئے۔	I We, You, They, He She, It did not eat pizza. میں نے پڑا نہیں کھایا۔	Pizza was not eaten by me. (us, you, him, her, it, them) پڑا مجھ سے نہیں کھایا گیا۔ (اگر پڑا جمع ہو) Pizzas were not eaten by me. (us, you, him, her, it, them) پڑا مجھ سے نہیں کھائے گئے۔

Interrogative Sentences سوالیہ جملے		Interrogative Negative سوالیہ منفی جملے	
Active Voice فعلِ معروف	Passive Voice فعلِ مجہول	Active Voice فعلِ معروف	Passive Voice فعلِ مجہول
Did I, we, you, they, he, she, it eat pizza? کیا میں نے پڑّا کھایا؟	Was pizza eaten by me? (us, you, him, her, it, them) کیا پڑّا مجھ سے کھایا گیا؟ (اگر پڑّا جمع ہو) Were pizzas eaten by me? (us,you,him,her,it, them) کیا پڑّا مجھ سے کھائے گئے؟	Did I, we, you, they, he, she, it not eat pizza? کیا میں نے پڑّا نہیں کھایا؟	Was pizza not eaten by me? (us,you,him, her,it, them) کیا پڑّا مجھ سے نہیں کھایا گیا؟ (اگر پڑّا جمع ہو) Were pizzas not eaten by me? (us,you,him, her,it, them) کیا پڑّا مجھ سے نہیں کھائے گئے؟

Past Continuous Tense
فعل ماضی جاری (زنانہ ماضی استمراری)

ہدایات: ۱- فعل مجہول (Passive voice) کے سبھی زمانوں میں فعل کی تیسری شکل (eaten) کا استعمال ہو گا۔

۲- اس زمانہ میں مفعول واحد کے ساتھ was being اور جمع مفعول کے ساتھ were being کا استعمال ہوتا ہے۔

۳- (Passive voice) کے سبھی زمانوں میں I کو me، we کو us میں، he کو him میں، she کو her، they کو them میں تبدیل کیا جاتا۔

Positive Sentences مثبتی جملے		Negative Sentences منفی جملے	
Active Voice فعلِ معروف	Passive Voice فعلِ مجہول	Active Voice فعلِ معروف	Passive Voice فعلِ مجہول
I, He, She, It was eating pizza. میں پڑا کھا رہا تھا۔	**Pizza was being eaten by me.** (us, you, him, her, it, them) پڑا مجھ سے کھایا جا رہا تھا۔ (اگر پڑا جمع ہو) **Pizzas were being eaten by me.** (us, you, him, her, it, them) پڑا مجھ سے کھائے جا رہے تھے۔	I, He, She, It was not eating pizza. میں پڑا نہیں کھا رہا تھا۔	Pizza was not being eaten by me. (us, you, him, her, it, them) پڑا مجھ سے نہیں کھایا جا رہا تھا۔ (اگر پڑا جمع ہو) Pizzas were not being eaten by me. (us, you, him, her, it, them) پڑا مجھ سے نہیں کھائے جا رہے تھے۔
We, You, They were eating pizza. ہم پڑا کھا رہے تھے۔		We, You, They were not eating pizza. ہم پڑا نہیں کھا رہے تھے۔	

Interrogative Sentences سوالیہ جملے		Interrogative Negative سوالیہ منفی جملے	
Active Voice فعلِ معروف	Passive Voice فعلِ مجہول	Active Voice فعلِ معروف	Passive Voice فعلِ مجہول
Was I, he, she, it eating pizza? کیا میں پڑا کھا رہا تھا؟	Was pizza being eaten by me? (us, you, him, her, it, them) کیا پڑا مجھ سے کھایا جا رہا تھا؟ (اگر پڑا جمع ہو) Were pizzas being eaten by me? (us, you, him, her, it, them) کیا پڑا مجھ سے کھائے جا رہے تھے؟	Was I, he, she, it not eating pizza? کیا میں پڑا نہیں کھا رہا تھا؟ Were we, you, they not eating pizza? کیا ہم پڑا نہیں کھا رہے تھے؟	Was pizza being not eaten by me? (us, you, him, her, it, them) کیا پڑا مجھ سے نہیں کھایا جا رہا تھا؟ (اگر پڑا جمع ہو) Were pizzas being not eaten by me? (us, you, him, her, it, them) کیا پڑا مجھ سے نہیں کھائے جا رہے تھے؟
Were we, you, they eating pizza? کیا ہم پڑا کھا رہے تھے؟			

Past Perfect Tense

فعلِ ماضی مکمل

ہدایات:۔1۔ فعل مجہول (Passive voice) کے سبھی زمانوں میں فعل کی تیسری شکل (eaten) کا استعمال ہو گا۔

2۔ اس زمانہ میں had been کا استعمال ہوتا ہے۔

3۔ (Passive voice) کے سبھی زمانوں میں I کو me میں we کو us میں he کو him میں she کو her میں they کو them میں میں تبدیل کیا جاتا۔

Positive Sentences مثبتی جملے		Negative Sentences منفی جملے	
Active Voice فعلِ معروف	Passive Voice فعلِ مجہول	Active Voice فعلِ معروف	Passive Voice فعلِ مجہول
I, We, You, They, He, She, It had eaten pizza. میں نے پزّا کھایا تھا۔	Pizza had been eaten by me. (us, you, him, her, it, them) پزّا مجھ سے کھایا گیا تھا۔	I, We, You, They, He, She, It had not eaten pizza. میں نے پزّا نہیں کھایا تھا۔	Pizza had not been eaten by me. (us, you, him, her, it, them) پزّا مجھ سے نہیں کھایا گیا تھا۔

Interrogative Sentences سوالیہ جملے		Interrogative Negative Sentences سوالیہ منفی جملے	
Active Voice فعلِ معروف	**Passive Voice** فعلِ مجہول	**Active Voice** فعلِ معروف	Passive Voice فعلِ مجہول
Had I, we, you, they, he, she, it eaten pizza?	Had pizza been eaten by me? (us, you, him, her, it, them)	Had I, we, you, they, he, she, it not eaten pizza?	Had pizza not been eaten by me? (us, you, him, her, it, them)
کیا میں نے پڑّا کھایا تھا؟	کیا پڑّا مجھ سے کھایا گیا تھا؟	کیا میں نے پڑّا نہیں کھایا تھا؟	کیا پڑّا مجھ سے نہیں کھایا گیا تھا؟

Simple Future Tense
فعل مستقبل مطلق

ہدایات:۔۱ اس زمانہ میں will be کا استعمال ہوتا ہے۔

۲۔ فعلِ مجہول (Passive voice) کے سبھی زمانوں میں فعل کی تیسری شکل (eaten) کا استعمال ہو گا۔

۳۔ اس زمانہ میں مفعول کو فاعل کی جگہ پر اور فاعل کو مفعول کی جگہ پر رکھا جاتا ہے اور اس سے پہلے by لگایا جاتا ہے۔

۔Passive voice) یہ) کے سبھی زمانوں میں I کو me میں we کو us میں he کو him میں she کو her میں they کو them میں میں تبدیل کیا جاتا۔

Positive Sentences مثبتی جملے		Negative Sentences منفی جملے	
Active Voice فعلِ معروف	Passive Voice فعلِ مجہول	Active Voice فعلِ معروف	Passive Voice فعلِ مجہول
I ,We shall eat pizza. میں پزا کھاؤنگا۔	Pizza will be eaten by me. (us,you, him,her,it, them)	I ,We shall not eat pizza. میں پزا نہیں کھاؤنگا۔	Pizza will not eaten by me. (us,you, him,her,it, them)
You, They, He, She It will eat pizza.	پزا مجھ سے کھایا جاینگا۔	You, They, He, She It will not eat pizza.	پزا مجھ سے نہیں کھایا جاینگا۔

53

Interrogative Sentences سوالیہ جملے		Interrogative Negative سوالیہ منفی جملے	
Active Voice فعلِ معروف	Passive Voice فعلِ مجہول	Active Voice فعلِ معروف	Passive Voice فعلِ مجہول
Shall I, we eat pizza? کیا میں پڑا کھاؤں گا؟	**Will pizza be eaten by me?** (us, you, him, her, it, them) کیا پڑا مجھ سے کھایا جائے گا؟	Shall I, we not eat pizza? کیا میں پڑا نہیں کھاؤں گا؟	Will pizza be not eaten by me? (us, you, him, her, it, them) کیا پڑا مجھ سے نہیں کھایا جائے گا؟
Will you, they, he, she it eat pizza?		Will you, they, he, she, it not eat pizza?	

54

Future Perfect Tense

فعلِ مستقبل مکمل

ہدایات:۔ 1۔ اس زمانہ میں will have been کا استعمال ہوتا ہے۔

2۔ فعلِ مجہول (Passive voice) کے سبھی زمانوں میں فعل کی تیسری شکل (eaten) کا استعمال ہو گا۔

3۔ اس زمانہ میں مفعول کو فاعل کی جگہ پر اور فاعل کو مفعول کی جگہ پر رکھا جاتا ہے اور اس سے پہلے by لگایا جاتا ہے۔

4۔ (Passive voice) کے سبھی زمانوں میں I کو me میں we کو us میں he کو him میں she کو her میں they کو them میں میں تبدیل کیا جاتا۔

55

Positive Sentences مثبتی جملے		Negative Sentences منفی جملے	
Active Voice فعلِ معروف	Passive Voice فعلِ مجہول	Active Voice فعلِ معروف	Passive Voice فعلِ مجہول
I, We Shall have eaten pizza. میں پزّا کھاؤں گا یا کھا چکوں گا۔	**Pizza will have been eaten by me.** (us, you, him, her, it, them) پزّا مجھ سے کھایا جا چکے گا۔ یا پزّا مجھ سے کھالیا جائیگا۔	I, We Shall have not eaten pizza. میں پزّا نہیں کھاؤں گا یا نہیں کھا چکوں گا۔	Pizza will have not been eaten by me. (us, you, him, her, it, them) پزّا مجھ سے نہیں کھایا جا چکے گا۔ یا پزّا مجھ سے نہیں کھالیا جائیگا۔
You, They, He, She It will have eaten pizza.		You, They, He, She It will have not eaten pizza.	

56

Interrogative Sentences سوالیہ جملے		Interrogative Negative سوالیہ منفی جملے	
Active Voice فعلِ معروف	Passive Voice فعلِ مجہول	Active Voice فعلِ معروف	Passive Voice فعلِ مجہول
Shall I, we have eaten pizza? کیا میں پڑا کھاؤں گا یا کھا چکوں گا۔	**Will pizza have been eaten by me?** (us, you, him, her, it, them) کیا پڑا مجھ سے کھایا جا چکے گا؟ یا کیا پڑا مجھ سے کھایا جائے گا؟	Shall I, we have not eaten pizza? کیا میں پڑا نہیں کھاؤں گا یا نہیں کھا چکوں گا۔	Will pizza have not been eaten by me? (us, you, him, her, it, them) کیا پڑا مجھ سے نہیں کھایا جا چکے گا؟ یا کیا پڑا مجھ سے نہیں کھایا جائے گا؟
Will you, they, he, she it have eaten pizza?		Will you, they, he, she it have not eaten pizza?	

Please do refer the link:

https://www.eslprintables.com/grammar_worksheets/verbs/verb_tenses/verb_tenses_charts/Verb_tenses_chart_370125/

Forms of verb

Verbs are words that show an action (sing), occurrence (develop), or state of being (exist). Almost every sentence requires a verb. The basic form of a verb is known as its infinitive. The forms call, love, break, and go are all infinitives. Almost all verbs have two other important forms called participles.

Verb comes from the Latin verbum, a word. It is so called because it is the most important part in a sentence. It is the word that tells or asserts something about a person or thing. Different forms of verbs are must to build a tense. Thus before the knowledge of tense - the base of English language - knowledge of three forms of verb - First form of Verb, Second form of Verb and Third form of verb - and its usages is must for the learner any language.

Present Tense	Past Tense	Past Participle	Present Participle
Abuse	Abused	Abused	Abusing
Act	Acted	Acted	Acting
Add	Added	Added	Adding
Admire	Admired	Admired	Admiring
Advise	Advised	Advised	Advising
Allow	Allowed	Allowed	Allowing
Answer	Answered	Answered	Answering
Appear	Appeared	Appeared	Appearing
Appoint	Appointed	Appointed	Appointing
Arise	Arose	Arisen	Arising
Arrest	Arrested	Arrested	Arresting
Arrive	Arrived	Arrived	Arriving
Ask	Asked	Asked	Asking
Attack	Attacked	Attacked	Attacking
Awake	Awoke	Awaken	Awaking
Bake	Baked	Baked	Baking
Bark	Barked	Barked	Barking
Bathe	Bathed	Bathed	Bathing
Be	Was were	Been	Being
Bear	Bore	Born	Bearing
Become	Became	Become	Becoming
Beg	Begged	Begged	Begging
Begin	Began	Begun	Beginning
Behave	Behaved	Behaved	Behaving
Behold	Beheld	Beheld	Beholding
Believe	Believed	Believed	Believing
Bend	Bent	Bent	Bending
Bet	Bet	Bet	Betting
Bid	Bade	Bidden	Bidding
Bind	Bound	Bound	Binding
Bite	Bit	Bitten	Biting
Bleed	Bled	Bled	Bleeding

Bless	Blessed	Blessed	Blessing
Blow	Blew	Blown	Blowing
Boast	Boasted	Boasted	Boasting
Boil	Boiled	Boiled	Boiling
Borrow	Borrowed	Borrowed	Borrowing
Break	Broke	Broken	Breaking
Bring	Brought	Brought	Bringing
Build	Built	Built	Building
Burn	Burnt	Burnt	Burning
Burst	Burst	Burst	Bursting
Buy	Bought	Bought	Buying
Call	Called	Called	Calling
Carry	Carried	Carried	Carrying
Cast	Cast	Cast	Casting
Catch	Caught	Caught	Catching
Change	Changed	Changed	Changing
Check	Checked	Checked	Checking
Choose	Chose	Chosen	Choosing
Clap	Clapped	Clapped	Clapping
Clean	Cleaned	Cleaned	Cleaning
Climb	Climbed	Climbed	Climbing
Cling	Clung	Clung	Clinging
Close	Closed	Closed	Closing
Collect	Collected	Collected	Collecting
Come	Came	Come	Coming
Complain	Complained	Complained	Complaining
Consult	Consulted	Consulted	Consulting
Cook	Cooked	Cooked	Cooking
Copy	Copied	Copied	Copying
Cost	Cost	Cost	Costing
Count	Counted	Counted	Counting
Cover	Covered	Covered	Covering
Creep	Crept	Crept	Creeping
Cross	Crossed	Crossed	Crossing
Crow	Crowed	Crowed	Crowing
Cry	Cried	Cried	Crying
Cut	Cut	Cut	Cutting
Dance	Danced	Danced	Dancing
Deceive	Deceived	Deceived	Deceiving

Decide	Decided	Decided	Deciding
Decorate	Decorated	Decorated	Decorating
Defeat	Defeated	Defeated	Defeating
Desire	Desired	Desired	Desiring
Die	Died	Died	Dying
Dig	Dug	Dug	Digging
Dip	Dipped	Dipped	Dipping
Discover	Discovered	Discovered	Discovering
Divide	Divided	Divided	Dividing
Do	Did	Done	Doing
Draw	Drew	Drawn	Drawing
Dream	Dreamed	Dreamed	Dreaming
Drink	Drank	Drunk	Drinking
Drive	Drove	Driven	Driving
Drown	Drowned	Drowned	Drowning
Dye	Dyed	Dyed	Dyeing
Earn	Earned	Earned	Earning
Eat	Ate	Eaten	Eating
Employ	Employed	Employed	Employing
Enter	Entered	Entered	Entering
Explain	Explained	Explained	Explaining
Face	Faced	Faced	Facing
Fail	Failed	Failed	Failiing
Fall	Fell	Fallen	Falling
Fear	Feared	Feared	Fearing
Feed	Fed	Fed	Feeding
Feel	Felt	Felt	Feeling
Fight	Fought	Fought	Fighting
Find	Found	Found	Finding
Fine	Fined	Fined	Fining
Finish	Finished	Finished	Finishing
Flee	Fled	Fled	Fleeing
Float	Floated	Floated	Floating
Fly	Flew	Flown	Flying
Forbid	Forbade	Forbidden	Forbidding
Forget	Forgot	Forgotten	Forgetting
Freeze	Froze	Frozen	Freezing
Gather	Gathered	Gathered	Gathering
Get	Got	Got	Getting

Give	Given	Given	Giving
Graze	Grazed	Grazed	Grazing
Grind	Ground	Ground	Grinding
Grow	Grew	Grown	Growing
Hang	Hung	Hung	Hanging
Hate	Hated	Hated	Hating
Have	Had	Had	Having
Hear	Heard	Heard	Hearing
Help	Helped	Helped	Helping
Hide	Hid	Hidden	Hiding
Hold	Held	Held	Holding
Hurt	Hurt	Hurt	Hurting
Improve	Improved	Improved	Improving
Invite	Invited	Invited	Inviting
Join	Joined	Joined	Joining
Jump	Jumped	Jumped	Jumping
Keep	Kept	Kept	Keeping
Kill	Killed	Killed	Killing
Kneel	Knelt	Knelt	Kneeling
Knit	Knitted	Knitted	Knitting
Know	Knew	Known	Knowing
Laugh	Laughed	Laughed	Laughing
Lay	Laid	Laid	Laying
Learn	Learned	Learned	Learning
Leave	Left	Left	Leaving
Lend	Lent	Lent	Lending
Let	Let	Let	Letting
Lie	Lay	Lain	Lynig
Light	Lit	Lit	Lighting
Like	Liked	Liked	Liking
Listen	Listened	Listened	Listening
Live	Lived	Lived	Living
Look	Looked	Looked	Looking
Lose	Lost	Lost	Listening
Love	Loved	Loved	Loving
Make	Made	Made	Making
Marry	Married	Married	Marrying
Mean	Meant	Meant	Meaning
Meet	Met	Met	Meeting

Melt	Melted	Melted	Melting
Mend	Mended	Mended	Mending
Mix	Mixed	Mixed	Mixing
Move	Moved	Moved	Moving
Name	Named	Named	Naming
Need	Needed	Needed	Needing
Nip	Nipped	Nipped	Nipping
Obey	Obeyed	Obeyed	Obeying
Open	Opened	Opened	Opening
Oppose	Opposed	Opposed	Opposing
Order	Ordered	Ordered	Ordering
Pay	Paid	Paid	Paying
Peep	Peeped	Peeped	Peeping
Plant	Planted	Planted	Planting
Play	Played	Played	Playing
Plough	Ploughed	Ploughed	Ploughing
Pluck	Plucked	Plucked	Plucking
Praise	Praised	Praised	Praising
Pray	Prayed	Prayed	Praying
Preach	Preached	Preached	Preaching
Prepare	Prepared	Prepared	Preparing
Prevent	Prevented	Prevented	Preventing
Promise	Promised	Promised	Promising
Prove	Proved	Proved	Proving
Pull	Pulled	Pulled	Pulling
Punish	Punished	Punished	Punishing
Push	Pushed	Pushed	Pushing
Put	Put	Put	Putting
Quit	Quit	Quit	Quitting
Quarrel	Quarrelled	Quarrelled	Quarrelling
Rain	Rained	Rained	Raining
Reach	Reached	Reached	Reaching
Read	Read	Read	Reading
Refuse	Refused	Refused	Refused
Remember	Remembered	Remembered	Remembering
Repair	Repaired	Repaired	Repairing
Reply	Replied	Replied	Replying
Resign	Resigned	Resigned	Resigning
Rest	Rested	Rested	Resting

Return	Returned	Returned	Returning
Ride	Rode	Ridden	Riding
Ring	Rang	Rung	Ringing
Rise	Rose	Risen	Rising
Roar	Roared	Roared	Roaring
Save	Saved	Saved	Saving
Saw	Sawed	Sawed	Sawing
Say	Said	Said	Saying
See	Saw	Seen	Seeing
Seek	Sought	Sought	Seeking
Select	Selected	Selected	Selecting
Sell	Sold	Sold	Selling
Send	Sent	Sent	Sending
Set	Set	Set	Setting
Shake	Shook	Shaken	Shaking
Shed	Shed	Shed	Shedding
Shine	Shone	Shone	Shining
Shoot	Shot	Shot	Shooting
Shrink	Shrank	Shrunk	Shrinking
Shut	Shut	Shut	Shutting
Sing	Sang	Sung	Singing
Sink	Sank	Sunk	Sinking
Sit	Sat	Sat	Sitting
Slay	Slew	Slain	Slaying
Sleep	Slept	Slept	Sleeping
Slip	Slipped	Slipped	Slipping
Speak	Spoke	Spoken	Speaking
Spend	Spent	Spent	Spending
Spit	Spat	Spat	Spitting
Spread	Spread	Spread	Spreading
Stand	Stood	Stood	Standing
Stay	Stayed	Stayed	Staying
Steal	Stole	Stolen	Stealing
Stick	Stuck	Stuck	Sticking
Stop	Stopped	Stopped	Stopping
Strike	Struck	Struck	Striking
Study	Studied	Studied	Stydying
Swear	Swore	Sworn	Swearing
Sweep	Swept	Swept	Sweeping

Swim	Swam	Swum	Swimming
Swing	Swung	Swung	Swinging
Take	Took	Taken	Taking
Talk	Talked	Talked	Talking
Teach	Taught	Taught	Teaching
Tear	Torn	Torn	Tearing
Tell	Told	Told	Telling
Think	Thought	Thought	Thinking
Thrust	Thrust	Thrust	Thrusting
Tie	Tied	Tied	Tying
Touch	Touched	Touched	Touching
Trust	Trusted	Trusted	Trusting
Try	Tried	Tried	Trying
Understand	Understood	Understood	Understanding
Use	Used	Used	Using
Wait	Waited	Waited	Waiting
Walk	Walked	Walked	Walking
Wander	Wandered	Wandered	Wandering
Wash	Washed	Washed	Washing
Waste	Wasted	Wasted	Wasting
Watch	Watched	Watched	Watching
Wear	Wore	Worn	Wearing
Weave	Wove	Woven	Weaving
Wed	Wedded/Wed	Wedded/Wed	Wedding
Weep	Wept	Wept	Weeping
Win	Won	Won	Winning
Wind	Wound	Wound	Winding
Wish	Wished	Wished	Wishing
Wonder	Wondered	Wondered	Wondering
Work	Worked	Worked	Working
Worship	Worshipped	Worshipped	Worshipping
Wound	Wounded	Wounded	Wounding
Wrap	Wrapped	Wrapped	Wrapping
Wring	Wrung	Wrung	Wringing
Write	Wrote	Written	Writing

Made in the USA
Columbia, SC
05 November 2023